CROCODILIANS

by Tanya Lee Stone

BLACKBIRCH®
PRESS

THOMSON

GALE

San Diego • Detroit • New York • San Francisco • Cleveland • New Haven, Conn. • Waterville, Maine • London • Munich

THOMSON

GALE

Photographs © 1994 by Chang Yi-Wen; pages 22-23 © corel

Cover photograph © PhotoDisc

© 1994 by Chin-Chin Publications Ltd.

No. 274-1, Sec.1 Ho-Ping E. Rd., Taipei, Taiwan, R.O.C.
Tel: 886-2-2363-3486 Fax: 886-2-2363-6081

Dedication: For Alan, Jake, and Liza

The author and publisher would like to thank Dr. Adam Britton
for his expert review of the manuscript and photographs.

LIBRARY OF CONGRESS CATALOGING-IN-PUBLICATION DATA

Stone, Tanya Lee.
  Crocodilians / by Tanya Lee Stone.
    p. cm. -- (Wild wild world)
Summary: Explores the behavior, physiology, eating habits, and other characteristics of crocodiles, alligators, and caimans.
Includes bibliographical references (p. 24).
  ISBN 1-4103-0037-4 (hardback : alk. paper)
  1. Crocodilians--Juvenile literature. [1. Crocodilians.] I. Title.
II. Series.

QL666.C9S76 2003
597.98--dc21

2003005144

Printed in Taiwan
10 9 8 7 6 5 4 3 2 1

Table of Contents

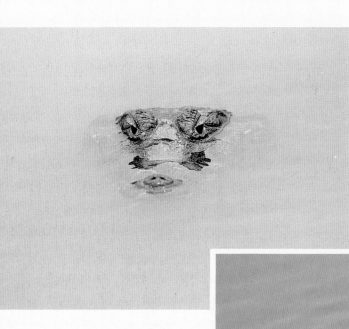

About Crocodilians

Crocodiles, alligators, and caimans belong to a group of reptiles called crocodilians. Their ancestors have been on the earth for 240 million years. These reptiles lived alongside the dinosaurs!

Crocodilians live in warm rivers and swamps around the world, including parts of the United States, Central America, South America, Africa, southern Asia, and Australia.

Some also spend time in saltwater. Alligators can survive in colder climates than most crocodiles.

There are many different kinds of crocodilians. But they share most things in common. They are intelligent animals that are covered in a scaly armor. They all have long snouts, and dozens of sharp teeth.

At Home in the Water

These huge reptiles are most at home in the water. Often, all that can be seen are the tops of their heads. They can stay hidden like this for hours until an animal either swims near or gets close to the water s edge. Then the reptile quickly springs into action to snatch its next meal!

Crocodiles, alligators, and caimans are excellent swimmers. Their long tails sweep side to side, which moves them through the water.

Their webbed feet also help them steer. A third, clear eyelid protects their eyes and allows them to see underwater. Unlike fish, crocodilians do not have gills. They breathe through their lungs and have to come to the surface for air.

The Crocodilian Body

Crocodiles, alligators, and caimans are fierce hunters. Fully grown, their powerful bodies weigh up to 3,200 pounds. A crocodilian can grow from 5 to 21 feet long. A tough, scaly, waterproof armor covers their neck and back. They have thick, soft, smooth skin on their belly.

Crocodiles, alligators, and caimans have long heavy, tails and strong legs. Their back feet have four toes and their front have five. The first three toes on each foot have sharp nails.

Crocodilians have a keen sense of sight and smell. Because their eyes and nostrils are placed on top of their flat head, they can see everything going on around them while hiding in the water.

Cold-Blooded

Like all reptiles, crocodilians are cold-blooded. This means that the temperature of their body changes with the temperature of the air or water around them. Being cold-blooded helps reptiles save energy. It also means they can survive when food is scarce.

To warm up, crocs bask in the sun or lie in warm, shallow water. They often live in small groups and can be seen soaking up the sun together. These reptiles often lie in the sun with their mouth open. Some scientists think is a way of heating up or cooling down.

Opening their mouth also shows off their sharp, white teeth! This sends an important message to other animals to leave them alone.

During the hottest part of the day, crocodilians often take to deeper, cooler water so they don t overheat. Or, they find shady spots where they can cool off on land.

Walking on Land

Crocodilians spend much of their lives in the water, but they have no trouble walking on land. Their short legs are strong and support their heavy bodies. Their webbed feet also help them walk on muddy, marshy land.

Even more amazing,
some kinds of crocodiles
can run really fast!

Expert Hunters

Crocodiles, alligators, and caimans are deadly hunters. Once they have an animal gripped in their jaws, there is little chance of escape. The muscles used to close their jaws are very powerful. Inside their mouths, they have sharp, fanglike teeth. These teeth come in different sizes, but they all have the same pointy shape.

Crocodilians do not waste time chewing their food. They crush it, tear it apart, and swallow it! Doing this, they often lose teeth. This is not a problem their teeth grow back!

Meat-Eaters

Hungry crocodilians will attack just about anything that comes within striking range. They are meat-eaters. They eat birds, turtles, frogs, and mammals.

They also eat a lot of fish. Some crocodilians fish in groups. They will make a dam with their bodies and trap large fish.

Some crocodiles can take down big mammals, such as zebras or wildebeests. They can do this with lightning-fast movement and the element of surprise. Once it snaps its jaws shut on its prey, a croc will quickly wrestle it into the water. Then it drowns the animal. Once the prey is dead, the crocodilian tears it apart and eats it.

Mating and Egg Laying

During breeding season, males will fight with other males over a female. Like other reptiles, crocodiles, alligators, and caimans hatch from eggs. A female prepares a nest for her eggs. Some build a nest of grasses and other plant materials on land to protect the nest from rising water. Others dig a shallow hole in sand near the edge of a riverbank. The eggs are laid in a hole inside the nest and covered over.

The female lays a clutch of 10 to 60 eggs. Each is about 2 to 4 inches long. But her nest is not safe. Hawks, ferrets, wild pigs, and even lizards will eat these eggs. (They will also eat young crocodilians.) To protect her eggs, a female guards her nest for more than two months. Even so, many eggs will be eaten before they can hatch.

When a baby is ready to hatch, it makes grunting and squeaking noises. It has a special egg tooth on the tip of its snout that helps slice open the tough shell. Hatchlings are about 8 to 12 inches long. Some mothers carry their young in their mouth to help them get from the nest to the water. Babies are able to swim right away.

Some caiman mothers take turns watching over the young of several mothers. The young stay close to their mothers for 2 weeks to 2 years.

Crocodilians and Humans

Adult crocodilians only fear other, large crocodilians and human beings. Many crocodilians have been hunted for their beautiful skin, and the meat of their tails. People also make expensive leather shoes, handbags, belts, and many other items out of crocodile and alligator skin.

In addition to being hunted, crocodilians have lost much of their habitat to building projects and farming.

Today, there are laws that protect crocodilians. These laws tell people which types of crocodilians are allowed to be hunted or farmed, and how many can be killed each year. It is illegal to hunt

certain kinds of these reptiles at all, such as the Chinese alligator. These controls help make sure that all of these amazing animals will continue to roam the earth for a long time to come.

For More Information

Perry, Phyllis J. *The Crocodilians: Reminders of the Age of Dinosaurs.* Danbury, CT: Franklin Watts, 1997.

Robinson, Claire. *In the Wild: Crocodiles.* Crystal Lake, IL: Heinemann Library, 1997.

Woodward, John. *Endangered! Crocodiles & Alligators.* New York: Marshall Cavendish, 1999.

Visit Dr. Adam Britton's website, www.crocodilian.com, to learn more about the natural history and conservationof alligators, crocodiles, and caimans.

Glossary

bask to warm up in the sun

clutch a group of crocodile eggs